O Donut! My Donut!

AND OTHER FUN POEMS

Jennifer Andrea

For anyone who needs a laugh

Table of Contents

I'd Just Like To Say

(Inspired by William Carlos Williams' "This Is Just To Say")

I have taken

your Porsche

that was in

the driveway

and which you

probably

waxed

yesterday.

Forgive me

for the dent

it was so fast

and so fun

The Toad Not Taken

(Inspired by Robert Frost's "The Road Not Taken")

A toad emerged from the mellow woods,
From underneath the undergrowth.
And me the hiker, long I stood —
Was on vacation and knew I could
Hang out a while, stop and loaf.

I sat on a log and tidied my hair,
Hoping that it would tell me its name
Because I was lonely while I was there.
He croaked two words; it was Jon Sinclair.
To me, he seemed rather peaceful and tame.

And he that morning to me did say,
He wanted to ride in my yellow backpack.
"Oh," I said, "you should probably stay,
Because the food at my house is super lame,
But I will look for you when I come back."

I am telling this story with a sigh:
Sometime ago a friendship commenced,
A toad emerged from the woods, and I —
I did not take the cute little guy.
And now it's time to go visit him.

Delight In This Latte

(Inspired by Robert Herrick's "Delight in Disorder")

A sweet espresso is the best;
It helps alleviate the stress.
To start your day, it gets you going,
Is a great distraction.
The work, the kids, the here and there.
I go, sometimes I don't know where.
The coffee shop is just nearby.
Baristas brew drinks on the fly.
The milk of choice is soy or oat.
I sit and I remove my coat.
I care less now, I'm on a high,
On chocolate curls and spicy chai.
The caramel, the milky heart,
Is really quite a work of art.

Looking At Food In A Company Fridge

(Inspired by Robert Frost's "Stopping by Woods on a Snowy Evening")

Whose lunch this is I think I know.
Her cubicle is in my row.
She will not see me standing here
To watch this meal with giddy glow.

My coworker would find it strange
To find the food that she'd arranged
Was missing, had completely vanished.
From the workplace kitchen fridge.

I reach inside and contemplate —
Ask myself if this is fate,
That I forgot my lunch today
Yet here is one that I can take.

The food is tempting, but I think
About the bills I have knee-deep.
And job I'd really like to keep,
And job I'd really like to keep.

Because I did not stop for Gas

(Inspired by Emily Dickinson's "Because I could not stop for Death")

I was driving, Mom beside —
Sis in the back seat —
Because I did not stop for gas —
The car stopped suddenly —

We coasted slow — a turtle's pace —
The Chevron far away —
A cloudy sky and overcast —
A very Portland day —

We barely cleared the Hawthorne Bridge —
And passed an urban hiker —
When on a single wheel rolls by —
Darth Vader Unipiper —

Out of the car — and with the help —
Of people passing by —
We pushed it to a nearby lot —
And left it for the night —

We walked some blocks to 5th and Clay —
While Mother made a fuss —
Then got some coffee for the road —
And took a TriMet bus —

The moral of the story is —
Make sure your car has fuel —
'Cause stranded on a boulevard —
Is really not that cool —

Henry

Henry is late.
He has a date.
That is the reason
he put on the skates.

Under the sky,
he's rolling by.
Nobody knows
if he's gay, straight or bi.

Rushing to meet
some cute lovely bird,
he earnestly hopes
they won't think him a nerd.

He chooses to travel
in curious ways.
For him it is skates
that is the big craze.

Not so much flying
or flitting around,
but one with the earth,
he is close to the ground.

Zen on the weekends.
Yoga at night.
And if he were able
he'd go fly a kite.

If he had a hand,
he'd carry some flowers
or smoke a cigar
while he drinks whiskey sours.

A nice one he is;
he'll help out another,
like take out the trash
for his sister or brother.

The one he is meeting —
the sweet little tweeter —
will come to find out
that this bird is a keeper.

To My Loudly Snoring Partner

(Inspired by Anne Bradstreet's "To My Dear and Loving Husband")

My deep sleep is interrupted
by what sounds like
jagged stones
tumbling down
a metal washboard
or
the staccato bark of
of a semi-truck's
Jake Brake
as it wends its way
downhill.
I gently nudge you,
to no avail.
I get up
and go to the couch.

Of The Funnel Cakes At The Fair

(Inspired by Ezra Pound's "In a Station of the Metro")

The saturation of grease in the batter;
Powdered sugar on a round airy cake.

I Almost Broke My Foot In A Gopher Hole

I was walking through the backyard,
to see if there was a ripe tomato,
when I stepped into a gopher hole.
I wobbled for a moment
and cursed the rodent
loud enough
for the neighbors to hear.
Then I got some dirt
and filled the hole
as I watched a carrot
slowly disappear into the earth.

My Cell Phone Fell Into The Ocean

I went to the beach one day
waded in the water
up to my knees.
When I bent over
to retrieve the dog's tennis ball,
my cell phone
that was in my shirt pocket,
fell into the ocean.
I pressed the power button
and got the "screen of death."
I let it dry
on the dresser.
Then half a year later
I pressed the power button
and it still worked!

To The Stoners, To Make The Most Of Time

(Inspired by Robert Herrick's "To the Virgins, to Make Much of Time")

Gather your dried buds while you can.
    I hope you won't be fearful.
For this green flower, banned today,
    Tomorrow will be legal!

The bright grow lamp has lit the weed,
    Nourished it to life.
The male plants all are ridded of,
    And now there's just the wife.

The time that's best for harvesting
    Is fall, when they're still young,
For if you let it grow too long
    Then it will be too strong.

So listen up; enjoy this time
    To smoke the sacred herb
'Cause one day Mom will get fed up
    And make you get a job.

The Passionate Dancer To Their Love

(Inspired by Christopher Marlowe's "The Passionate Shepherd to His Love")

Come dance with me my precious love,
And we will moonwalk to the Louvre.
We'll cha cha in the nearby fields,
And jazzy dance like Jennifer Beals.

A polka in our wooden crocks,
On hardwood floors in just our socks.
We'll square dance to the caller's calls,
And waltz all night at fancy balls.

We'll tango — in our mouths red roses,
And vogue all night in striking poses,
Hike up our pants, sashay like Urkel,
Then dance with lobsters when we snorkel.

A two-step in a banquet hall,
A conga with my Uncle Paul,
We'll dance to warm us when we're cold,
And boogie like on *Solid Gold*.

Electric Slide with all our buds,
A schottische in our boots with studs,
We'll hip hop to the funky groove,
And slow dance when we fall in love.

We'll tap dance like smooth Ben Vereen,
And Zumba every May morning.
If you're like me and live to move,
Then dance with me and be my love.

Making Peace With My Pizza Belly

It might look like I'm
five months pregnant,
but I'm not!
It's just that
I eat too much
ice cream
and
pizza
and
donuts
and
pizza
and
funnel cakes
and
pizza
and
elephant ears
and
pizza
and
churros
and
pizza.
I can't blame it on my thyroid.
It's just that I'm too lazy
to go to the gym.
Plus,
I'm always
at the carnival

so that doesn't help.
Therefore,
I've decided to
make peace
with my pizza belly.

Wine, How I Love You

(Inspired by Elizabeth Barrett Browning's "How Do I Love Thee?")

Wine, how I love you. I will count the ways.
I love the bold Chiantis and the creamy Chardonnays.

A spritzy wine for lunch, a Riesling for the night.
A sommelier shall pair the food with wine that is just right.

I love the dry Merlots. Adore the sweet bouquets.
I'm joyful when they come around with wine in carafés.

I love the bubbly flirty wine that's often drunk with brunch.
I love Sangria mixed with fruit and served as "happy" punch.

Ice wine at the barbecue, mulled at Christmas-time.
A Confetti pink Moscato with a tangy twist of lime.

Baguettes brushed with olive oil, plates of charcuterie,
A sip of fortified vermouth — a great aperitif!

"Wine gives strength to weary men," as Homer one time said.
I drink you in the hot tub and I drink you in my bed.

Some Norah Jones or Boyz II Men, a glass beside the fire,
And if I could drink wine at work, that is my one desire.

True happiness wine brings my life — and if I have my way,
I'll drink a toast to Zinfandel and Rosé every day!

If we were going to the mall

(Inspired by Emily Dickinson's "If you were coming in the fall")

If we were going to the mall,
I'd kiss the cats goodbye
With half a can of tuna fish,
So kitties would not cry.

If we would wear our tennis shoes,
The ones with little balls —
We'd count our steps with tracking apps,
In air-conditioned halls —

If we could catch a Macy's sale,
I'd fill my bag with shoes,
Or at the Barnes & Noble store
Some books I would peruse.

If certain that my credit card —
Had not surpassed its limit,
I'd top my bag with Cinnabon,
And later would consume it —

But now you sleep, and it's too late.
You lie on sheets of flannel.
I'll have to lounge with kitty cats —
And watch The Shopping Channel —

Alas, I Have Stinky Gas

I have stinky gas today.
It smells like rotten eggs.
It seeps out from my anus
and warms up both my legs.

When I'm in the elevator
or I'm chatting with a friend,
I clench my butt cheeks super tight
So that I will not offend.

I cough and hope a louder noise
will cover up the sound,
but if it doesn't work,
I sometimes blame it on the hound.

When I'm cutting veggies,
I also cut the cheese.
I'm good at multitasking
'Cause I pass gas while I sneeze.

It might sound like a duck
or a deflating balloon,
or a trumpet or a tuba
or a French horn or bassoon.

What food might I be eating
that is causing this foul odor?
Could it be the burgers
or the donuts or the soda?

I fart when I'm asleep.
I'm wakened, then I curse.
I fan the sheets to rid the smell
but that just makes it worse.

To be a lot less gassy,
I really must try harder;
at home they now call me
The Incredible Serial Farter.

What my bottom needs
is an exhaust control device
like a catalytic converter
to make the noxious fumes smell nice.

I pop a pill for gas
because I'm gagging on my stench.
I hope that come tomorrow
I will have less flatulence.

Pollen Is Out To Get Me

My antibody warriors
are no match for
these microscopic dragons.
I rub my eyes
until my corneas ache,
yet the itching persists.
I go to get a tissue
but the snot
is faster than I
and lands
on my shirt
and onto the floor.
My head feels like
a crew of elves
inside, banging,
with tiny elf sledgehammers.
I swallow an allergy pill,
tilt my head over the sink,
squirt saline solution
into my sinuses,
then drink nettle tea
with a dollop
of honey.
I lie on the couch,
weak, moaning —
wondering
how something so miniscule
can wreak so much havoc.

Song Of Portland

(Inspired by Walt Whitman's "Song of Myself")

I celebrate a sacred land
One of indigenous nations
Multnomah, Clackamas, Tualatin
Tribes of the Portland Basin

It sits at the foot of majestic Mt. Hood
Near the end of the Oregon Trail
The one on which Sacajawea traversed
With Lewis and Clark and detail

It garnered its name when two dudes tossed a coin
Asa Lovejoy was hoping for Boston
Since Pettygrove won, it isn't called that
But instead it's been christened as Portland

Willamette River divides the town's east side from west
Burnside Street splits the north from the south
So much love of diversity of the four sections
That is really what Portland's about

Southeast has Oaks Park, Bagdad Theater, OMSI
Northeast—the street fair, Beverly Cleary walking tour
Southwest has the zoo, arboretum, Voodoo Doughnut
Northwest—Alphabet District, Forest Park, shopping galore

It's the City of Roses, a city of bridges
All the nicknames reveal ingenuity
Portlandia, Stumptown, P-Town, PDX
And Beervana for all of the breweries

It's a town that makes sense, numbered streets go in order
Roundabouts help maintain traffic flow
At the crosswalk you stop if you see someone crossing
Those on foot have permission to go

Vibrant life in downtown — orchestra at the Schnitzer
Christmas tree at the Pioneer Square,
naked bike rides, parades, some historic hotels
Portland State University's there

From the old Pittock Mansion, in the West Hills of Portland
One can witness a breathtaking view
Powell's Books boasts vast floor space, with colorful rooms
And thousands of titles for you

At the Waterfront Park, catch a blues festival
Board a boat for a bountiful brunch
Walk the Tilikum Bridge, ride the Aerial Tram
At the Saturday Market have lunch

Moda Center is where Nine Inch Nails has performed
It's the home of the Portland Trail Blazers
Eat a jumbo "Blaze" dog from the concession stand
Watch as Lillard shoots awesome three-pointers

You can leave all the hubbub and stroll amongst flowers
Where the Rose Garden has an assortment
On the outskirts of town, there is hiking and camping
And fishing for endless enjoyment

In the spring one wears pants, in the summer it's shorts
During autumn it's sandals with socks
Since the winters are cold, it is better with layers
When you're warm, you can peel each one off

Whether coming or going, at the Portland Airport
Note the teal carpet's fanciful shapes
It's a testament to the uniqueness, the pride
The elan of this wonderful place.

i carry these bags with me, in my trunk

(inspired by e.e. cummings' "[i carry your heart with me (i carry it in]")

i carry these bags with me, i carry them in
my trunk. i am never without them, anywhere
i go, they go. it's clear; whatever shopping is done
you see, is with these bags, my bags
                                these here

no waste, this is our world, it is sweet. i want
this earth to last, this green and blue
and it's yours too — whatever we make it
reduce, reuse, recycle; less carbon footprint

here is my deep dark secret nobody knows:
i hate to carry these freaking bags.
they pop out of my trunk or sometimes
i forget them and have to walk back to my car.
it's a wonder i can even hold a job, yet,
i carry these bags, i carry them in my trunk

O Donut! My Donut!

(Inspired by Walt Whitman's "O Captain! My Captain!")

O DONUT! My Donut! The baking is now done.
The oven's weathered scorching racks, and now it's time for fun.
The moment near, car alarms I hear, the people all are bustling,
And follow eyes with steady gaze, the manager slowly rustling.

    But O sugar! Sugar! Sugar!
    I've gotten out of bed,
    For comfort food I need right now,
    I will be aptly fed.

O Donut! My Donut! Rise up and hear the cash register.
Rise up — for you the coffee's made — for you the insulin taken.
For you children skip and old men hobble — for you the parking
lot is crowded.
For you they call, the addicted masses. Your virtues have
been touted.

    Here Donut! Dear donut!
    As Homer Simpson said,
    "Mmm… donuts."
    I will be aptly fed.

My Donut does not answer. Its surface iced and still.
My sweet orb does not feel my hand. It has no pulse or will.
The Camry is park'd safe and sound; the key is in my pocket.
I give up thanks and break the bread. There's nothing that can
top it.

Exalt O S'mores, and Oreos!

Ding Dongs and pumpkin bread,

For in my hand the donut lies.

I will be aptly fed.

The Ubiquitous Dog Hair

Our dog is super hairy,
his nickname German Shedder.
We bathe him and we brush him,
yet there's dog hair everywhere!

There's dog hair on the carpet.
There's dog hair in my shoe.
There's dog hair on the sofa.
There's dog hair in my food!

I give the dog a hug;
there's dog hair on my shirt.
I use the rolley sticky thing
before I go to work.

I clean behind the fridge,
I find a wad of hair.
I open up a book to read,
there's dog hair even there!

I go into the yard to pick
a luscious ripe blueberry.
I'm shocked to find the tiny fruit
not smooth but rather hairy.

We vacuum and we sweep.
Put dog hair in a sack.
But this is rather pointless,
because he shakes and it's right back.

Sometimes I wish we had instead
a beagle or a poodle
or a hamster or a rabbit
or a precious golden doodle

or a goldfish or a parrot
or just anything less hairy
like a chicken or a piglet
or a ferret or canary.

If dog hair were a fuel
it would rapidly be sold.
If shedding an Olympic sport
our dog would win the gold.

You'd think with so much shedding
all his hair would go away,
and he would need a parka
or a sporty tan toupee.

If there could be a way
to package all the hair,
and if rich eccentrics wanted it
I'd be a millionaire!

For some the dog hair's useful;
little birds will take the tufts
and use it for their nests.
It's good the hair's ubiquitous!

Chilaquiles

With a package corn tortillas,
and some salsa and some cheese,
then you have the items
for a meal to really please.

Check tortilla package
if you're going gluten-free.
Just omit the cheese
to make this dinner dairy-free.

Cut up corn tortillas;
if for you, then three or four,
into bite-sized squares.
If there's a party, cut up more.

Heat a pan on medium.
Pour some oil to coat the bottom.
Then add the cut tortillas,
stirring often 'til they soften.

Sprinkle in some salt.
And if you like a little crunch,
then cook a tad bit longer
for a very yummy lunch.

Add a quarter cup of salsa
or amount that you desire.
Stir until well-mixed,
then remove it from the fire.

Sprinkle queso fresco
or your choice of grated cheese.
Put it on a plate
and arrange it as you please.

Then gobble it all up.
And be surprised with which the ease,
you made this tasty dish.
As you can see, it is a breeze.

The Green Go Light

(Inspired by William Carlos Williams' "The Red Wheelbarrow")

so much rides

upon

a green "go"

light

at the drag

races

before the revving

cars

Salsa

Boil 3 tomatoes — Roma the best one,
in a pot half-full of water.
They start to peel,
that means they're done.

Pour out all the water.
Let tomatoes cool.
Place them in a blender.
Now begin to drool.

Add a clove of garlic,
or maybe make it two,
if the smell of garlic breath
doesn't bother you.

Sprinkle in some salt,
or to give a little punch,
add a dash of pepper flakes.
Be careful, not too much.

Drain the excess water,
after placing lid askew.
Then press the lid on tight,
and pulse until it's smooth.

Pour it in a bowl.
Set the bowl aside.
Dice a quarter onion.
This might make you cry.

If you like cilantro,
chop a little bit.
Add this and the cut-up onion
to tomato mix.

If you want it creamy
or to make a little more,
stir in some tomato sauce
you've gotten from the store.

Now the salsa's ready.
You can eat it with some chips,
or mash some avocado,
add some salsa; make it dip.

If your beans are bland,
make them more exciting!
Add some scrumptious salsa.
Your legumes will be delighting.

When you're beating eggs to scramble,
add a little bit,
or to a grilled cheese sandwich
it can give an extra kick.

Spanglish

(Inspired by Rudyard Kipling's "If")

If you light your candles

with *mechas*,

If you *parquear* your *troca*

in the *parqueadero,*

If half of your sentence is Spanish

and the other half English, as in, *Que cute,*

If you like *crutones*

in your salad,

If you eat your *lonche*

every day at noon,

If you save money because

you *cuponear,*

If you're computer savvy

and know how to *twitear* and *googlear,*

If you have good credit because

you pay your *biles* on time,

If you eat *panqués* for breakfast

and glazed or maple *dónas* for dessert,

If you place a Spanish article in front of an English phrase

as in, *Los Chicken McNuggets,*

If your entire sentence is in English except for two words

as in, I'm going to *la pulga* this weekend,

If your piggy bank is full of

nicles and *daimes,*

If you go to the gym because you have too much

yonque in the *tronque,*

If you say to someone with a wheelbarrow

Púchale!

If you pay your *renta*

on time every month,

If you say to a reckless driver

Wátchale!

Then you my dear

speak Spanglish!

Ita And Ito

To make a Spanish word
a bit endearing or *diminutivo*,
remove a letter or two from the end
and add the suffix —ita or —ito.
Juana becomes *Juanita*.
Sara is *Sarita*.
Lola is *Lolita*.
Concha is *Conchita*.
A gato is *gatito*,
a perro a *perrito*,
a bird is *pajarito*,
a baby monkey, a *changuito*.
If you're just a smidgen fat
because you eat too much *sopita*,
you don't have to say you're *gorda*.
You can say you're just *gordita*.
"C" becomes "qu,"
which makes a taco a *taquito*.
Someone skinny is *el flaco*,
but if you love him, he's *flaquito*.
"Z" becomes a "c,"
which makes Lorenzo, *Lorencito*.
G becomes "*gu*,"
which makes amigo, *amiguito*.
Exception to the endings —
Remove the "o" and add an "*ita*;"
if it's "hand," then it's "*la mano*,"

but if it's tiny, "*la manita*."
A donkey is a *burro*,
but the food is a *burrito*.
If you like the happy hour
you can sip a cool *mojito*.
If a woman's name is Margaret,
it converts to *Margarita*,
which is too, the word for daisy
or a drink made with tequila.
A daughter is *mijita*.
A son is called *mijito*.
The hero's name is *Juarez*
his first name is *Benito*.
Some words need no letters removed:
Manuel is *Manuelito*,
and a baby dinosaur would be a
brontosaurusito.

Mosquito, Be Not Proud

(Inspired by John Donne's "Death, be not proud")

Mosquito, be not proud. While some may deem you

Mighty and scary, it is not so;

For those you think you can simply land on,

Protest. Poor mosquito, you can't bite me either.

My days and nights are disturbed by your buzzing.

Much nuisance; so from here you really must go,

The sooner the better, and flies and gnats should go too.

Bug me no more you annoying little pest.

Thou art smitten with the legs and arms of nude sleepers,

And your poison makes us itch.

Spiders and murder hornets make us miserable as well,

And worse than you, so what do you think?

One swift swat or squirt of citronella

And you shall bite no more! Mosquito, you shall die!

Prayer To The Chicken Gods

Dear chicken Gods,

Thank you for eggs:

Hard-boiled eggs

Soft-boiled eggs

Egg drop soup

Egg salad sandwiches

Deviled eggs

Easter eggs and cascarones

Over-easy eggs

Over-medium eggs

Sunny-side up eggs

Scrambled eggs

Huevos rancheros.

Thank you for eggs to make these things:

Oatmeal cookies

Cornbread

Lemon meringue pie.

I'm sorry I broke those 3 eggs

At the grocery store;

I'm clumsy.

Thank you for soft baby chicks.

Thank you for my neighbor's chickens

She gives us eggs sometimes

And the yolks are really yellow.

By the way,

Why don't chickens fly?

Thank you for chicken bouillon

And chicken noodle soup
Especially on a cold blustery day.
Thank you for fried chicken
Roasted chicken
Chicken parmigiana
Chicken cacciatore
Chicken teriyaki
Chicken chow mein
Chicken fajitas
Chicken enchiladas
Arroz con pollo
Chicken skewers.
Roosters are a little annoying
But thank you for them anyway.
I suppose if we didn't have clocks
They'd come in handy.
Thank you for silly jokes, such as,
"Why did the chicken cross the road?"
And for silly sayings such as,
"There's no one here but us chickens."
Thank you for the chicken dance
That I do at Oktoberfest every year.
Thank you for wishbones;
I think they're really cool.

Xanadu

(Inspired by Samuel Taylor Coleridge's "Kubla Khan")

A muse
sent to inspire
A scintillating kiss
Olivia Newton-John's
heavenly voice
Gene Kelly sashaying
across a
dance floor
Pink leg warmers
Gold skates
Black boots
Cream ribbons
Glitz
Magic
Sparkle
A hopping night club
Nine sisters tap dancing
on a revolving
kaleidoscope stage
A skating party
Cowboy hats
Teetering tight-rope walkers
Transformations
Dreams that come true

Working In The Yard On A Lovely Day

(Inspired by Robert Frost's "Stopping By Woods on a Snowy Evening")

Whose poop this is, I think I know.
His house is down the street. Although,
I did not see him stopping here,
To watch my yard fill up with turds.

Between the heather and the soil,
What I touch makes me recoil.
The slimy log one left behind
Negates the joy of all my toil.

The little dog has no regard;
He always doo doos in my yard.
The owner should have waste bag handy.
Next time I will be more on guard.

My yard was lovely; now I weep,
But I have excrement to heap,
And piles of poop before I sleep,
And piles of poop before I sleep.

I Hear The Baseball Fans Singing

(Inspired by Walt Whitman's "I Hear America Singing")

I HEAR the baseball fans singing, various songs I hear.

Those of the parents cheering on their little leaguers.

Fans of the Cardinals, Yankees, Royals,

Dodgers fans rooting for Kershaw to throw fastballs and sliders,

Fans at Fenway Park, whooping when Wally the Green

Monster yells,

    "Play ball!"

Fans of Mookie Betts, singing, hoping he'll steal a base,

so we can have a free taco at Taco Bell,

Tampa Bay fans rooting for Arozarena as he stumbles,

then gets back up and makes a miraculous homerun,

Fans eating delicious hot dogs or roasted peanuts or ice cream

out of

    mini Chicago Cubs helmets,

Each singing for their favorite in the All-Star game,

The World Series belongs to whomever wins it.

Fans are singing with open mitts hoping to catch a flyball,

    but sometimes they're a bit tipsy and fall over.

To Fish Or Not To Fish

(Inspired by William Shakespeare's Hamlet)

To fish, or not to fish, that is the question:
Whether 'tis better to stand near this river
And hope that a salmon lands in my mouth
Or to forage in town for Cheetos and bear claws.

ABOUT THE POEMS

Realizing I needed more education if I wanted to succeed at creating a well-written memoir about my childhood, I decided at age 48, to go back to school. Portland State University accepted me into their creative writing program. While the emphasis of my bachelor's degree was nonfiction, one of the required classes was an introduction to poetry, which I took in the summer of 2019. "O Donut! My Donut!" was written as part of an assignment for that class. After reading it to the professor and other students, amid laughter, someone shouted, "You should totally publish that!" I said, "Okay, I will" (not thinking I actually would).

Over the next several months, I wrote parody poems, as well as poems wholly of my own creation, as a way to relax in between school terms. When I'd written 27, I decided I was ready to publish the compilation. I looked online for how many poems are necessary to publish a book of poems and found a website that stated a minimum of 30 is needed.

So, I quickly conjured up what I call "filler poems" to bring the total to 30. They are: "Prayer To The Chicken Gods," "I Hear The Baseball Fans Singing" and "The Passionate Dancer To Their Love." The latter actually took me a year and a half to write. I started writing it in that introduction to poetry class, but could only manage to eke out two lines. I was trying to place the poem in France because "Louvre" was the only suitable word I could find to rhyme with Christopher Marlowe's "prove." I tried and gave up on that poem several times, the difficulty being that I've never been to Paris so I couldn't imagine the landscape of where a dancer might flit about. Finally, I was able to finish the poem by making it about dancing in general.

"Prayer To The Chicken Gods" came after I accidentally broke three eggs at the grocery store due to my innate clumsiness. Feeling guilty for breaking the eggs, I asked someone what to do and they suggested I ask forgiveness of the chicken gods. I loved the idea so much, I decided to write a poem about it.

Jennifer Andrea

"I Hear The Baseball Fans Singing" spawned from watching the 2020 World Series in which Randy Arozarena stumbled, got back up and miraculously made a homerun.

With "Chilaquiles" and "Salsa," I thought it would be fun to transform recipes into poems. It was quite challenging however, to keep in mind the ingredients, the steps of the recipe, the meter and the rhyme.

"Because I did not stop for gas" is a shout-out to a place near and dear to my heart: Portland, Oregon. When I read this poem for a group of people in the spring of 2021, it was more well-received than I had expected. So, I decided to write another more lengthy poem about this spectacular place titled, "Song Of Portland," a parody of Walt Whitman's "Song of Myself," making it the thirty-first and penultimate poem written for this collection.

During the publishing process, I decided to write one more poem titled, "To Fish Or Not To Fish," a parody of William Shakespeare's "To be, or not to be," soliloquy from the play Hamlet. From my local library, I checked out some books about bears, intending to compose an elaborate poem about polar bears, panda bears and black bears. But after writing one simple stanza told from a grizzly bear's perspective, I decided the poem was complete.

Except for the e. e. cummings and Emily Dickinson parodies, all of the words in the titles of my poems are capitalized. This was a purposeful aesthetic choice.

Juji generously generated extremely cute, tender drawings to accompany the poems. The painting of Henry, the bird on roller skates, was actually done by Juji years ago. I wrote the poem "Henry," in response to it. The other drawings were created in response to the poems.

I wanted to keep the book light and happy. I also wanted everyone to be able to relate to the poems. Justin Grinnell, during one of our critique sessions, noted that in the poem "O Donut! My Donut!" I had "gendered" the donut. The donut originally was a "he," since the captain in "O Captain! My Captain!" is a "he." But I changed the "he" to "it," to make the donut more relatable to everyone. Hopefully I've accomplished that.

Jennifer Andrea
Dundee, Oregon, July 2021

GRATITUDE

First, a very special thank you goes to my mother, Janie Peña Menchaca, for passing on to me her love of the poetry of Robert Frost and Emily Dickinson.

A huge thank you goes to Juji Smith, for the cute heartfelt drawings that accompany the poems.

Thank you Julie Schoening, for convincing me to go back to school.

I'd like to extend gratitude to my amazing instructors of poetry and literature at Portland State University, who introduced me to such marvelous works: Professor Elisabeth Ceppi, Professor Tracy Dillon, Professor Tom Fisher, Professor Jessica Hiestand, Professor Susan Reese and Professor Christine Rose. Also, thank you Professor Rachel Noorda and Professor Stephanie Argy for imparting your wisdom about the book publishing industry.

I am super grateful to my Portland State University classmates for waking up early on Saturdays and sharing their valuable critiques: Justin Grinnell, Aydia Johnson and Isabel Rekow.

Thank you Cherry City Writers and 9 Bridges, for your helpful insight.

Thank you Cole Bowman, for your thorough edits.

Thank you Kelly Davidson, for suggesting times to publish this book. Timing really is everything.

Thank you Muse, for pouring creative energy into me.

Thank you Rachel Kerr, Zachary Johnson and the entire BookBaby team, for being a vital part of making this dream come true.

Thank you readers, for your investment in this book.